Who Is
Shaquille O'Neal?

by Ellen Labrecque

illustrated by Manuel Gutierrez

SCHOLA

To my Ursinus College friends and teammates—
all of them champions in my heart and mind—EL

In memory of my father,
Francisco Gutierrez—MG

A Note from the Publisher

At Who HQ, a dedicated team of authors, illustrators, editors,
designers, and fact-checkers strive to bring you the very best books
about trailblazers, legends, famous places, and world-shaping events.
It's our goal to tell each story accurately and keep our facts up-to-date,
and we work with experts to review our content and language.
The history we tell is vital, and the way we tell it is just as important.

We firmly believe history lives in the facts and we recognize the
different points of view of our readers from all around the world.
We consistently review our books and rely on readers like you
to help us tell these stories in the correct way.

No part of this publication may be reproduced, stored in a retrieval system, or transmitted
in any form or by any means, electronic, mechanical, photocopying, recording,
or otherwise, without written permission of the publisher. For information regarding
permission, write to Penguin Workshop, Permissions Department, 1745 Broadway,
15th Floor, New York, NY 10019.

ISBN 978-1-339-00742-7

Text copyright © 2022 by Ellen Labrecque. Illustrations copyright © 2022 by
Penguin Random House LLC. All rights reserved. Published by Scholastic Inc.,
557 Broadway, New York, NY 10012, by arrangement with Penguin Workshop, an
imprint of Penguin Young Readers Group, a division of Penguin Random House LLC.
PENGUIN is a registered trademark and PENGUIN WORKSHOP is a trademark
of Penguin Books Ltd. WHO HQ & Design is a registered trademark of
Penguin Random House LLC. SCHOLASTIC and associated logos are trademarks
and/or registered trademarks of Scholastic Inc.

The publisher does not have any control over and does not assume any responsibility for
author or third-party websites or their content.

12 11 10 9 8 7 6 5 4 3 2 1   23 24 25 26 27 28

Printed in the U.S.A.   40

First Scholastic printing, January 2023

Contents

Who Is Shaquille O'Neal?

It was February 7, 1993, and the Orlando Magic were playing the Phoenix Suns in a National Basketball Association (NBA) game. The NBA is a men's professional basketball league that plays in North America. The Magic were only in their fourth season in the NBA. Their game was being broadcast live on national television for the first time in franchise history while a sold-out crowd of over nineteen thousand fans watched the game in the Suns' America West Arena. Everybody was focused on rookie Shaquille O'Neal, the Magic's seven-foot-one, three-hundred-pound center. Shaq (pronounced "Shack") played basketball like a bulldozer. In a game filled with giants, Shaq was *still* taller and stronger than his opponents. Defenders who got in his way could end up on the floor, or in the third row!

"When he gets the ball under the basket, I pray he misses," said Hakeem Olajuwon, another seven-foot-tall NBA center. "He's so big and he can't be stopped."

In the matchup against the Suns, Super Shaq did not disappoint his fans. Less than three minutes into the game, he went up for a thundering two-

handed dunk. The "Shaq attack" did not just bring down the rim and the backboard; it also pulled down the entire basket structure—the rim and net, the six-foot-by-three-foot backboard, and the bar and post the backboard and rim were attached to—onto the court. Players scattered out of the way to safety. No one had ever seen anything like it. No other player had ever had the strength and power to do something like that.

The game had to be delayed for thirty-seven minutes as workers brought in a whole new basket replacement. Shaq stood on the sideline and smiled a giant thousand-watt smile. He's a serious basketball player, but he knows how to have fun while playing the game, too.

"I was a little surprised," he said later about the mighty dunk. "But when it started coming down, I started running the other way."

Shaq finished the game with twenty points, but the Magic lost the game 121–105. The score didn't really matter, though. The Hercules-size dunk announced to the world that twenty-year-old Shaquille O'Neal was Superman in a basketball uniform. He was a star like no other.

CHAPTER 1
An Army Kid

Shaquille Rashaun O'Neal was born on March 6, 1972, in Newark, New Jersey. His mother explained that "Shaquille Rashaun" is an Arabic name that means "little warrior." (As he grew up, Shaquille's name sometimes got shortened to *Shaq* by family and friends.)

Shaquille was less than eight pounds at birth—an average weight for a baby. Shaquille's mother, Lucille O'Neal, was six feet, two inches

Lucille O'Neal with baby Shaquille

tall. She was eighteen years old when her son was born. Shaquille's father, Joseph Toney, was a couple years older than Lucille, and an inch shorter. When Shaquille was only six months old, Joseph left Newark; he was later sent away to jail. At first, Lucille raised Shaquille with help from women in her family. But when her son was two years old, Lucille married Philip Harrison.

Philip Harrison

Philip was an army reserve sergeant. By the time Shaquille was four years old, he was a head taller than other kids his age. When Lucille went out with her son, she had to make sure people treated Shaquille like a toddler and not like an older child.

Because of Philip's job in the army, Shaquille and his family moved around a lot. (On average, military families are relocated every three years because some members of the military require new training while others often achieve new positions.) When Shaquille was five, his family moved from Newark to Bayonne, New Jersey. When he was in third grade, the family moved to Fort Monmouth in Eatontown, New Jersey.

Moving was hard on Shaquille. He had to try to make new friends repeatedly. He was lonely much of the time. Watching cartoons helped him adjust to each new move. His favorite character, Superman, was always there for him.

During this time, Lucille and Philip had three children together—two daughters, Lateefah and Ayesha, and a son, Jamal. Shaq was a great big brother and always looked out for them.

"My mom taught me to change diapers, powder them, everything," said Shaq.

Philip's army training made him strict with the children, but especially with Shaquille. Sometimes Shaquille goofed off in school, trying to impress new friends. Philip would go to the school to make sure his stepson was paying attention and behaving. When Shaquille did something wrong, Philip would spank him to make sure he didn't do it again.

Kids teased Shaquille for being so tall. They called him names like Shaquilla the Gorilla or Big Foot. They told him that he was probably dumb and had been held back because he was so much bigger than anybody else. Shaquille got into fights because of all the teasing.

"My parents told me to be proud [of my size], but I wasn't," Shaquille said. "I wanted to be normal."

The one place Shaquille felt at home was at the local Boys and Girls Club in whichever town the family was living. He went every day after

school until his mom and dad came home from work. Going to the club gave Shaquille something to do with his time. It also helped him stay out of trouble. Shaquille did his homework, played games, and spent time doing a lot of different sports, including basketball. Shaq wasn't any good yet. He just liked playing.

"I was clumsy," Shaquille said. "I hadn't really grown into my body. Of course, everybody expected me to excel because I was so big. Good luck explaining to people it doesn't work that way."

By age eleven, Shaquille was already six feet, four inches tall. The average height for an eleven-year-old boy is almost two feet shorter. Shaquille had to stop trick-or-treating on Halloween because of his size.

Boys and Girls Clubs of America

The Boys and Girls Clubs of America is an organization that provides after-school programs for children all over the United States. The clubs—mostly run in school buildings—offer sports, homework help, reading, arts and crafts, and computer time.

The organization was started over one hundred years ago to provide a safe, fun, and productive way to spend time after school. Today, nearly four million children are members of the 4,300 clubs across the United States.

"When I would go to the door," Shaquille said, "people would just stand there, looking at me with their eyes wide open. 'You too big to be trick-or-treating, ain't you?'"

In the middle of his fifth-grade year, Shaquille's stepdad was transferred again, this time to Fort Stewart in Hinesville, Georgia.

After a short stay in Georgia, Shaquille and his family moved again to an army base in Wiesbaden, Germany, in 1984. Although Shaquille didn't know it at the time, his basketball career was just about to take off.

CHAPTER 2
Germany

There wasn't much for Shaquille to do in Germany. He was in a whole new country where it snowed a lot and people spoke a different language. Shaquille still showed off in school to help make new friends. One day, he tried to teach his classmates how to break-dance. Many American kids were doing these acrobatic hip-hop moves, but some of the kids from Germany had never seen them before. When Shaquille got on the ground to demonstrate a move, the teacher thought he was sick, or having a seizure!

She called his parents to come and take him to the doctor, but they knew Shaquille was fine. He practiced break-dancing around the house all the time.

When Shaquille wasn't dancing, he continued to help his mom with his brother and sisters. Shaquille loved being around younger kids. He loved playing with them and having fun. He nicknamed himself "Shaq Daddy."

Shaquille also spent a lot of time playing basketball. His stepfather practiced with him, doing one-on-one drills and teaching him to shoot and play defense. By the time Shaquille was

thirteen years old, he was six feet, eight inches tall. But he still wasn't that great at basketball and wasn't even playing on an organized team.

"I couldn't jump over a pencil," Shaquille said. "I couldn't run or shoot. I had to practice."

One day, an American college basketball coach visited the army base to run a basketball clinic—a meeting where basketball players are evaluated and given instruction—for local kids. Shaquille went to the clinic, too.

The man's name was Dale Brown, and he was

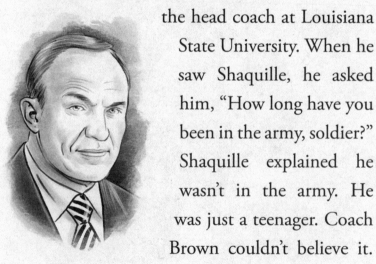

the head coach at Louisiana State University. When he saw Shaquille, he asked him, "How long have you been in the army, soldier?" Shaquille explained he wasn't in the army. He was just a teenager. Coach Brown couldn't believe it.

Dale Brown

He knew a kid this size could be a great basketball player one day if he worked hard.

During Shaquille's sophomore year of high school, his family was transferred back to the United States. They moved to San Antonio, Texas. All this moving was both good and bad for Shaquille. It was difficult because he had to adjust to a new school again and again. Moving so often can be hard—especially for a kid who didn't blend in with everybody else. However, moving so much was also good for Shaquille. It helped him become comfortable around strangers. It made him outgoing. He loved to joke and make other people smile. This was a trait that would stick with him his whole life.

"We made friends easier and quicker and adapted to new situations simply because we had to," Shaquille explained about himself and his siblings. "It was a survival tool."

CHAPTER 3
Star of the State

In 1987, Shaquille went to Robert G. Cole High School in San Antonio, Texas. He arrived from Germany too late to play for their basketball team as a sophomore, so he had to wait until his junior year. By 1988, at age sixteen, Shaquille was six feet, ten inches tall. All his daily practice habits from Germany had helped him become a much smoother player. He felt more comfortable with his height. He was athletic and powerful. Believe it or not, Shaquille still couldn't dunk the basketball, though. Basketball hoops are ten feet off the ground, and players a lot shorter than Shaq can dunk easily.

Shaq's new coach, Dave Madura, began
working with Shaq to help him jump higher. He
made Shaq do squats—crouching and standing
up with heavy weights on his shoulders—until
his legs felt like they were on fire. Then a friend of
Shaq's started working with him to dunk, asking
him to first dunk a sock. When Shaq could do
that, he gave him a tennis ball, then a softball,

then a volleyball, until finally he handed him a basketball. Once Shaquille learned to dunk, he couldn't stop.

Shaquille began working even harder on his game. He played a lot with the enlisted men who lived on the army base, since some of these men were a little closer to his size.

When Shaquille wasn't playing basketball, he watched it on television.

"I'd sit back and watch Michael Jordan and [Patrick] Ewing and take all sorts of mental notes,"

Michael Jordan

Patrick Ewing

Shaquille said about watching the former NBA stars. "Now when I closed my eyes, I wasn't dreaming about the Hulk or Superman anymore. I was dreaming about Ewing and Jordan."

Shaq became a national star during his two seasons at Cole High School. He was the biggest and toughest high school player anybody had ever seen. Newspapers around the country wrote about how great he was. His games were sold out every night. Little kids lined up and asked

him for autographs. College coaches came to his practices and games to try to get him to come to their schools. His teammates began calling him "Shaquille the Deal." By his senior year, Shaquille was offered more than one hundred college basketball scholarships! That meant he could study at a university for free if he committed to playing basketball for the school's team.

Shaquille loved all the attention. Maybe too much. He bragged a lot to his teammates and acted like he could win the games all on his own. One day, instead of practicing, Shaquille stood on the sidelines talking to a girl. Coach Madura told Shaquille to get on the court and run.

"Coach made me run until I almost threw up," said Shaq.

Shaquille soon changed his ways. He still loved to joke around, but only at the right time and place.

During his senior year in 1989, Shaquille

averaged thirty-one points, twenty-two rebounds, and eight blocked shots per game. He led his team to the Texas state championship title— their first one in school history. After the season,

Texas state basketball championship, 1980

he was named the co-Most Valuable Player (MVP) of the elite McDonald's High School All American Games, scoring eighteen points, grabbing sixteen rebounds, and blocking six shots. He was one of the best players in the country!

Shaquille chose to attend Louisiana State University (LSU), coached by Dale Brown. Coach Brown was the man Shaquille had met while his family was living in Germany. They had kept in touch, writing letters back and forth over the years. Dale Brown promised Shaquille he would teach him to be one of the world's best basketball players. He also promised he would teach him to be a good student and a good man.

"I just want you to know I'm recruiting a human being first and a basketball player second," Coach Brown told Shaquille's stepfather.

Shaquille became a good student. Even though he hoped to play professional basketball one day, he still wanted to get an education, too. LSU seemed like a school where he could do both things well.

CHAPTER 4
Tiger Years

Shaquille had to learn to adjust his game once he arrived at Louisiana State University in 1989. He wasn't the only star anymore; the Tigers already had a lot of good players. There were upperclassmen on the team who were better and more experienced than Shaquille.

"I thought I was The Man," Shaquille said. "What I realized when I got to LSU was that everyone there was The Man."

Coach Brown was just as strict and tough with Shaquille as Shaquille's stepdad had been. If Shaquille or any of the other players missed class, they had to get up at five thirty in the morning and go running. Coach Brown also gave all his players keys to the gym. This meant they

could go and practice on their own whenever they wanted to do so. Shaquille used his key a lot. When his teammates went to a party, he headed to the gym and practiced his game instead.

Coach Brown also asked a former NBA player, Kareem Abdul-Jabbar, to work with Shaquille in practice. Kareem was seven feet, two inches tall and

Kareem Abdul-Jabbar

one of the best centers to ever play the game. Fans started to wonder whether Shaquille could one day be as good as Kareem, who was famous for his hook shot, had won three National Collegiate Athletic Association (NCAA) titles at the University of California, Los Angeles (UCLA), and went on to become one of the highest scorers in NBA history. Kareem saw it differently. "Don't call Shaquille the next anybody," warned Kareem. "Let him be the first Shaquille."

Shaq really looked up to Kareem, and even chose to wear the number 33—the same number Kareem wore. During Shaquille's freshman year, he blocked 115 shots—a Southeastern Conference record! The Southeastern Conference is a group of colleges—mainly located in the Southeast part of the United States—that compete against each other in a variety of sports. Shaq's record was the sixth highest total in the country. He also led the conference in rebounds per game (12.0), ranking ninth in the country. Shaquille did well in the classroom, too. He finished the year with a 3.0 grade point average, a solid B. This was the highest average on the team.

Kareem Abdul-Jabbar (1947–)

Kareem Abdul-Jabbar (born Ferdinand Lewis Alcindor Jr.) played basketball for UCLA, where he led the team to three straight national championship titles. He perfected his famous skyhook—a one-handed shot that involves him releasing the ball from the highest possible point while using his body to shield the defender—in college because the NCAA did not allow players to dunk. In 1969, he was the number one pick in the NBA Draft and played for the Milwaukee Bucks. He would later play for the Los Angeles Lakers.

In his twenty-year career, Kareem won six NBA championship titles and was a six-time NBA MVP. He was inducted into the Basketball Hall of Fame in 1995.

Shaq practiced hard during the summer between his freshman and sophomore seasons. He played pickup basketball for three hours a day. At night he did calf raises to make his legs stronger, something he had been doing since high school. He also worked on new moves, like a baby hook shot.

When he came back to school as a sophomore, Shaquille had increased his vertical leap by eight inches in one summer. He could now dunk the ball over any opposing player.

"Shaq may be unguardable," said one opposing coach. "This guy may have the physical talent and personal discipline to be the best," said another.

Shaquille was now seven feet, one inch tall and weighed 294 pounds. He was nearly impossible to push around. He led the nation in rebounding, averaging 14.7 per game and ranked seventh in the nation in scoring. He also blocked 140 shots, a national record for college sophomores.

The Associated Press news syndicate named him the National Player of the Year. The Tigers shared the conference title that year with Mississippi State University.

Articles in newspapers and magazines started to name Shaquille the best center on the planet. Shaquille loved being in the spotlight and bragged about himself a lot. He always did it with a big wink and a smile, though, like he was sharing an inside joke with the world. Shaquille had nicknames for everything, including his celebration dances. He wore a black baseball cap with "I AM THE SHAQNIFICENT" written on

it. He stayed up late into the night listening to music and even creating new songs. He liked to rap for fun and sometimes talked in rhyme.

As a junior, Shaquille was the nation's leading shot blocker and ranked second in rebounding. Unfortunately, LSU lost in the second round of the NCAA tournament.

Shaquille decided not to return to LSU for his senior year. Instead, he entered the NBA Draft. Shaquille promised his mom he would eventually go back and complete his college degree. But for now, he was ready to join a professional team.

The NBA Draft

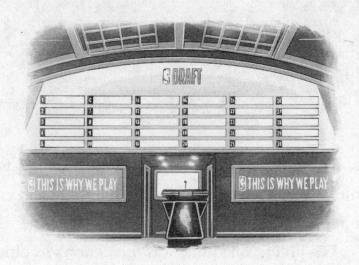

The NBA Draft takes place every June or July. The thirty NBA teams each draft, or select, college and international players to join their squad the following season. The teams with the worst record the previous season get the top picks in the draft. Since 1989, the draft has had two rounds. In total, sixty players are picked. Players are drafted not just from the United States but from all over the world.

CHAPTER 5
Magic Man

Now that Shaquille declared he was entering the NBA Draft, the NBA's general managers (the people who run the NBA teams) all said they would pick Shaquille if they got the chance. In 1992, the Orlando Magic team based in Orlando, Florida, got to pick the first player in the draft lottery.

On June 24, the NBA Draft took place in Portland, Oregon. Shaquille O'Neal was there with many of his closest friends and family. He called the group his "Love Shaq." The league commissioner, David Stern, stood behind a microphone and announced, "With the first

1		SHAQUILLE O'NEAL
2		
3		
4		
5		
6		
7		

pick in the NBA Draft, the Orlando Magic pick Shaquille O'Neal!" The room burst out in applause. Shaq gave a big smile, looked into the television camera and said, "Who, me?" He was joking, of course. Shaq knew he would be picked first.

Shaquille flew down to Florida the following

day. He was greeted at the airport by large groups of fans, lots of balloons, and the Orlando Magic cheerleaders and dancers. Shaq put on a pair of Mickey Mouse ears and gave a big grin. "I couldn't believe the greeting I got when I landed. People were jamming the airport terminal," Shaquille said.

Shaquille signed a contract with the Magic that paid him $41 million over the next seven years. He picked the number 32 jersey (33, his college number, was already taken, so he tried to get as close as he could). At the time, this was the biggest rookie contract in any sport. He also signed a deal with the sneaker company Reebok, which paid him $3 million to wear and promote their sneakers. Shaquille was given his own Reebok shoe called the Shaq Attaq. Each pair of

his sneakers would sell for $135! This was also the biggest sneaker contract ever for a rookie athlete. Shaquille had not played one second in a professional game, and he already had more money than he had ever imagined. This was mostly because he was so good at basketball. It was also because he was such a likable man. Many professional athletes were grim and serious. But Shaquille always looked like he was having fun.

Shaquille went home to San Antonio to get
ready for the upcoming season. But first he took
one day to celebrate. He went on the slides at
Splashtown, a waterpark in the area, with friends
from high school. Shaquille was a multimillionaire,
but he was still a big kid at heart.

Filling Shaq's Shoes

The average grown man wears a size 10.5 shoe, but Shaquille wears a size 22! His shoes are about sixteen inches long, but most companies don't make shoes this size. Reebok made Shaquille a new custom pair for every game. Shaquille also gets his regular shoes and everyday clothes specially made. The typical suit for a man requires 4½ yards of cloth. Shaq's suits require 7¼ yards!

Shaq's feet are tied for the biggest to ever play in the NBA. Center Bob Lanier, who played in the NBA in the 1970s and 1980s, was six feet, eleven inches tall and also wore size 22.

Shaquille played in his first NBA game on November 6, 1992. The Magic beat the Miami Heat by a score of 110–100. Shaquille had twelve points, eighteen rebounds, and three blocked shots. And he only got better as the season went on.

He became the first rookie to start an All-Star Game since Michael Jordan in 1985. Players in the All-Star Game are voted on the team by fans and players, and Shaq received the fourth highest number of votes, even though he was only a rookie.

Throughout the season, Shaquille continued to show off his fun side. He went on a talk show and rapped for the crowd. When he went to dinner in Orlando, or when he visited other cities for games, he always gave fans the biggest smile as he signed autographs.

Michael Jordan (1963–)

Michael was a star player at the University of North Carolina and was drafted to the Chicago Bulls in 1984. He played in the NBA until 2003 and won six NBA titles with the Chicago Bulls. Like Shaquille, Michael was as famous off the basketball court as he was on it. The Nike company created a sneaker line called Air Jordans. They are the best-selling sneakers of all time. The sports drink Gatorade created one of the catchiest advertising songs ever called "I (Wanna Be) Like Mike." Many people say Michael Jordan is the greatest basketball player ever. He played like he could fly, jumping higher and staying in the air longer than any other player.

Michael Jordan entered the NBA Hall of Fame in 2009.

Shaq's monstrous dunks became famous. During his rookie season, he brought two entire baskets—the rim, the backboard, and the entire post—down onto the court. No player had ever done this before. The first time he did it was in his first nationally televised game. The second time it happened, the Magic's radio announcer *still* couldn't believe his eyes.

"He brought it down! He brought the whole goal down!!!" the announcer screamed into his microphone as he watched Shaquille's dunk unfold.

The Magic went 41–41 during Shaquille's rookie season. He helped the team win twenty more games than it had the previous season. Shaquille was named the NBA Rookie of the Year.

CHAPTER 6
Superman

Shaquille's second season in the NBA was even better than his first. He finished second in the league in scoring, and the Magic went 50–32, making the playoffs for the first time in team history.

In the fall of 1993, Shaquille took his love of rap and turned it into a side career. He released his first rap album, *Shaq Diesel*. The album sold more than one million copies. He also starred in a college basketball movie titled *Blue Chips* and appeared in many commercials for

Reebok and Pepsi soda. Shaq was doing it all—
playing basketball, dancing, singing, and acting.

Shaquille lived his everyday life in a big way,
too. He bought a mansion in Orlando that was
twenty-three thousand square feet. Shaquille's
house had a pool, a full-size indoor basketball
court, a giant soda machine, and all kinds of
video games.

After he turned pro, Shaquille tattooed
a Superman logo on his left bicep. He even
nicknamed himself Superman. And just like his

favorite superhero, Shaquille liked helping people. He bought a new home for his mom, stepdad, and siblings in Orlando. He wanted his family nearby while he played. He stopped by often for his mom's home cooking.

He also bought houses for both sets of his grandparents. He liked to slip $100 bills to people who were living on the street. He visited sick kids in the hospital. Over Christmas, he dressed like "Shaq-a-Claus" and delivered toys to kids in poor neighborhoods.

"My parents taught me to give back," Shaquille said. "It was understood that if I became rich and famous like we thought I would, then I would share the wealth."

But just like Superman, Shaquille also had one weakness . . . making free throws. Slamming the ball through the hoop with three defenders hanging on his back was no problem for Shaquille—but shooting uncontested from fifteen feet away became a source of frustration. Once other teams realized he struggled from the free-throw line, they began to foul him more and more. At times, this was the only way defenders could stop him. This type of defense strategy even had a name—*Hack-a-Shaq*. When Shaquille was fouled, he got to go to the free throw line to shoot two shots. Even though these shots were unguarded, Shaquille could only manage to sink about half of them. (The top free-throw shooters in the league made more than 90 percent of their shots.)

The Magic's shooting coach worked with Shaquille all year. They tried to fix his shooting form. Nothing worked. Unfortunately, Shaquille would struggle with foul shooting his entire career.

Despite this flaw, Shaquille's time in Orlando was magical. In the 1994–1995 season, Orlando had the best record in their conference and made it all the way to the NBA Finals before losing to the Houston Rockets in four straight games. Off the court, he released three more rap albums and starred in another movie. In *Kazaam*, Shaquille played a three-thousand-year-old genie who was released from a boom box (a large portable radio) to grant a boy three wishes. *Kazaam* wasn't popular with critics, and it wasn't very successful, but Shaquille was still happy he made it. "I'd go through airports, and kids would run up to me and shout

'Kazaam!' with the biggest ole smiles on their faces, and it made me laugh. Every time," he explained.

Shaquille missed twenty-eight games in the beginning of the 1995–1996 season because he had a broken thumb. The Magic still made it to the NBA playoffs, but lost in the conference finals to Michael Jordan and the Chicago Bulls.

Shaq plays against Michael Jordan, 1996 NBA Playoffs

There were starting to be whispers that Shaq was great, but he couldn't win an NBA championship.

At the end of the 1995–1996 season, Shaq decided to opt out of his contact with the Magic and become a free agent. This meant he could sign again with Orlando or any other team for even more money. Every team wanted Shaquille, and they were willing to pay a lot to get him.

CHAPTER 7
Go West, Young Man

The Los Angeles Lakers offered Shaquille $120 million over seven years to come and play for their team. It was the highest contract in the history of the NBA at that time. For a man who loved to rap and star in movies, Los Angeles was

the perfect place. A lot of movies and music albums are made in Hollywood, a neighborhood of Los Angeles. On July 18, 1996, Shaquille accepted the offer. He was now officially a Laker.

Shaquille also joined the United States basketball team at the 1996 Summer Olympics in Atlanta, Georgia. Shaquille was thrilled to play for a gold medal in Atlanta. The 1996 United States team, filled with other NBA stars, won their games by an astounding average margin of 32.3 points. They easily beat Yugoslavia for the gold medal, 95–69.

Along with winning an Olympic gold medal, Shaq also hit another milestone that summer. He became a parent alongside his girlfriend, Arnetta Yardbourgh. Their daughter, Taahirah, was born on July 19, 1996. Shaq loved being a dad. He recorded his voice saying, "Daddy's right here," so his baby could hear his voice while he was away.

Despite enjoying his new role as a father, Shaquille had a rough time during the first three

seasons in Los Angeles. On the basketball court, he was injured and missed a lot of games. Off the court, Shaquille made a superhero movie called *Steel* that came out in the summer of 1997. He made another rap album that came out in September 1998. Neither the movie nor the album won any awards. But Shaq didn't mind too much because he was doing something he loved. Shaquille and Arnetta were also no longer a couple. Shaq began dating another woman named Shaunie Nelson.

Shaunie Nelson

The Lakers made it to the playoffs in Shaq's first three seasons, but they never made it to the NBA championship. Sports fans, writers, and television and radio announcers criticized Shaquille. They questioned if he was ever going to lead his team to an NBA title. They pointed out that he had not won a national championship in college, either. Some fans and sports writers blamed Shaquille for spending too much time making movies and rap albums, and not enough time practicing basketball. Shaquille worried about winning a championship, too.

"After three years in LA, none of my dreams about getting a ring were even closer to coming true," he said.

Shaquille didn't want to be the best player on teams that couldn't win a championship.

CHAPTER 8
A Champion

In the summer of 1999, the Lakers hired a new coach named Phil Jackson. Phil had been the head coach of the Chicago Bulls from 1989 to 1998. He led the Bulls to six NBA titles.

Phil Jackson

Shaquille was thrilled Phil Jackson was now the Lakers' coach. Phil explained to Shaquille that he had to get in better physical shape. Coach Jackson also reminded Shaquille basketball is a team game. Shaquille couldn't win by himself. It was the same message Shaquille's high school coach had told him years earlier.

Coach Jackson wanted Shaquille to get along with one teammate in particular—Kobe Bryant. Kobe was just as big of a star as Shaquille. But Kobe was six years younger and was more serious on and off the court. Shaquille would laugh and joke

Kobe Bryant

around with his teammates on bus rides. He would do raps off the top of his head. Kobe sat with his headphones on and quietly listened to music.

The stars did have one thing in common, though. They both *really* wanted to win the title. Shaquille and Kobe put their differences aside during the 1999–2000 season. The Lakers won sixty-seven games during the regular season. This was the most the Lakers had won in twenty-eight years. Shaquille averaged 29.7 points and 13.6 rebounds per game and was named the league's Most Valuable Player for the first time. Around this time, Shaquille and Shaunie also had a son together, Shareef.

Kobe Bryant (1978–2020)

Kobe Bryant was drafted into the NBA right out of high school in 1996. He played for the Los Angeles Lakers throughout his twenty-year career and won five NBA championships, led the league in scoring two times, and was named an All-Star eighteen times.

After Kobe retired from basketball in 2016, he ran his own entertainment production company and won an Academy Award for an animated short film he wrote called *Dear Basketball*. Kobe also owned his own training facility for young athletes.

On January 26, 2020, Kobe died in a helicopter crash along with his thirteen-year-old daughter, Gianna (called Gigi), and seven others. Kobe's fans mourned the loss of one of the most exciting athletes to ever play in the NBA.

During the NBA playoffs, Shaquille played even better than he did during the regular season. The Western Conference Finals between the Lakers and the Portland Trailblazers came down to Game Seven. After a slow start in the final game, Shaquille came alive in the fourth quarter. On one memorable play, Kobe lobbed the ball way up high for Shaq to dunk. The lob came down behind Shaquille. In one swift motion, Shaq reached behind his head with his right hand, grabbed the ball, then slammed it into the basket. The crowd went wild. The Lakers went on to win the game and the series, four games to three.

Shaquille called it "the greatest dunk and highlight of my career."

Three days later, the Lakers faced the Indiana Pacers for the championship. In Game One, Shaquille scored forty-three points and grabbed nineteen rebounds and the Lakers won easily. After the game, a reporter asked Shaquille how

he would guard himself. Reporters loved to ask Shaquille questions. He gave funny answers. This time Shaquille responded, "I wouldn't. I'd just fake an injury and go home."

The Lakers eventually won the Finals series, four games to two. Shaquille was awarded the NBA Finals MVP. More importantly, he was finally a champion.

Shaquille and Kobe gave each other a big hug after the final game. Their differences didn't matter for the moment; they were both champions.

Famous Lakers fans, like Jack Nicholson and Will Smith, also gave Shaquille hugs. "Everybody loves a winner," Shaquille concluded. "And nobody could say ever again that Shaq couldn't win the big one."

CHAPTER 9
Two More

Now that Shaquille had his championship ring, he wanted something to go with it—a college diploma! When he left Louisiana State University, he promised his mom he would go back and get his degree one day. Over the years, Shaq had been taking classes in the off-season. He finally earned his degree on December 15, 2000.

"I've very proud of him," Shaquille's mother, Lucille, said. "He made a promise to me, he set his goal, and he achieved it."

Shaquille joked around at his graduation. He said LSU stood for Love Shaquille University. After receiving his degree, he teased, "I feel secure I can get a real job now." He was also serious about how important his education was. "I have a lot of money," Shaquille said. "But I wouldn't be able to handle it without an education."

The college graduate continued to school his opponents on the court, too. The Lakers won the NBA championship for the second straight season in 2001. Shaquille averaged over fifteen rebounds and thirty points during the playoffs. He was named the NBA Finals MVP after the Lakers beat the Philadelphia 76ers for the title, four games to one. In the final championship game, he scored twenty-nine points, grabbed thirteen rebounds, and blocked five shots. Shaquille was double-teamed a lot. He overpowered not just one defender, but two.

"He's awesome, stupendous, fabulous, and dominating," said Shaquille's teammate Ron Harper. "I know that is the same thing I say about him every game, but what else is there to say?"

In the fall of 2001, Shaq's family was also growing bigger. He and Shaunie had a second child together, a daughter named Amirah.

In the 2002 NBA playoffs, the toughest series the Lakers faced was in the Western Conference Finals against the Sacramento Kings. Shaquille scored forty-one points (and even made thirteen of seventeen free throws) to help the Lakers come from behind to win a crucial Game Six.

During the NBA Finals, the Lakers faced the New Jersey Nets. Game Three was played in New Jersey, and Shaquille bought eighty tickets for his friends and family who lived nearby in Newark.

He now lived in a mansion in California, but he didn't forget where he grew up, either. With all his friends and family watching, Shaquille averaged 36.3 points per game and was named the NBA Finals MVP for the third year in a row. They swept the Nets in four games, becoming only the fifth team in NBA history to "three-peat" or win three titles in a row. Teammate Kobe Bryant came up to him after the game and said, "Congratulations, Greatest." Shaquille responded to Kobe, "Congratulations, Most Dominant."

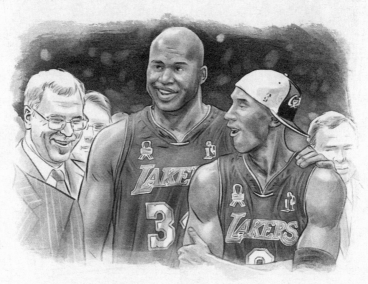

CHAPTER 10
A Fair Trade

In December 2002, Shaquille and Shaunie got married. In April 2003, their third child and second son, Shaqir, was born.

The Lakers won fifty games during the 2002–2003 regular season, but lost to the San Antonio Spurs in the Western Conference Semifinals. Shaquille wasn't just training for basketball all season, though. He had also enrolled himself in the Los Angeles Port Police Academy! Ever since Shaquille was a kid, he wanted to be a police officer. He had two uncles who were officers, and his stepdad was an army sergeant. On some days, Shaquille would go right from practice to the police academy for training!

Soon after the season ended, Shaquille was sworn in as a reserve police officer. Reserve police officers are volunteers, but they receive the same training and work alongside full-time officers.

"It was a lot of work, but I absolutely loved it," Shaquille said about his law enforcement training. Shaquille loved to do things for others, and he thought being a police officer was a great way to help people. Shaq knew, though, the one police job he'd never be able to do . . . work undercover!

Shaquille played through the 2003–2004 with an injured toe. The Lakers finished the regular season with a 56–26 record. They made it back to the NBA Finals, but lost to the Detroit Pistons, four games to one. The defeat was disappointing for the Lakers, and the season had been difficult, especially because Shaquille and Kobe fought a lot. When Shaquille joined the Lakers in 1996,

Kobe had been an eighteen-year-old rookie who started only six games all season. It was Shaquille's team—but now, Kobe had become the Lakers' leading scorer, and he expected Shaquille to share the spotlight. Shaquille thought Kobe was a ball hog who shot the ball whenever he wanted. Shaquille didn't want to play on the same team as Kobe anymore. He demanded to be traded.

On July 14, 2004, Shaq was traded to the Miami Heat. The Heat gave the Lakers three players and two draft picks just to get Shaquille.

Lakers fans were disappointed to lose their favorite man, but Miami fans were thrilled. Shaquille, now age thirty-two, guaranteed he would win a championship title for the team. He also joked, "I'm like toilet paper, Pampers, and toothpaste. I'm definitely proven to be good."

Miami fans loved him. Over four hundred number 32 jerseys (Shaquille's number) were sold on the team's website in the first two hours they became available. Shaquille was officially a Miami man now.

CHAPTER 11
A Fourth Ring

After breaking up with Kobe and the Lakers, Shaquille had something to prove, and his first season in Miami was his best in a couple years. The Heat won fifty-nine games, led by a healthy Shaquille and shooting star Dwyane Wade.

Dwyane Wade and Shaq, 2004

Whereas Shaquille and Kobe had fought over the ball, Shaquille and Dwyane seemed to like sharing it. Their first season together had many highlights, but they lost to the Detroit Pistons, four games to three, in the Eastern Conference Finals. Shaq played in seventy-three games, the most since 2001, and made his twelfth All-Star Game in a row.

Shaquille bought another giant house when he moved to Miami.

Usually when Shaquille would buy a house, he had to make construction changes to it so that it fit his size. But Shaquille bought this house from a former seven-foot NBA player. The showers and ceilings were already tall enough for Shaquille.

The following 2005–2006 season, Shaquille and Dwyane led the Heat to their first NBA title. They beat the Dallas Mavericks, four games to two. This was now Shaquille's fourth NBA title.

"Everything I had promised the city of

Miami had come true," Shaquille said. "We won a championship, we owned the city, and I had proven I could win anywhere."

In the spring of 2006, Shaq and Shaunie welcomed their fourth child together, a daughter named Me'arah. In the summer of that year, Shaquille went over to China to sell his own brand of sports clothes. Basketball is one of the most popular sports around the world, and China has the second largest fan base behind the United States. Speaking to a big crowd in Beijing, Shaquille bowed and said, "Hello. I'm Shaquille O'Neal and I love China." The people in China loved him right back. Journalists and fans followed him everywhere he went. Shaquille was having a great time.

Some teammates and fans back in Miami were unhappy with Shaquille. They thought he shouldn't be traveling; he should be getting ready for the season. Shaquille disagreed.

Shaq surrounded by fans while visiting
the Great Wall in China, 2006

"I can't hide who I am just because some people don't think I'm serious enough," he said. "When it comes time to take care of business, I'm going to take care of business. When it's time for fun, I'm going to have fun."

This is how Shaquille lived his entire life. Unfortunately, though, the following season wasn't any fun for Shaquille or the Heat. Shaquille missed fifty games of the regular season because of a knee injury. In true Shaquille fashion, he still found some time to amuse himself and his fans. At a practice session for the All-Star Game in February 2007, Shaquille started break-dancing at center court like he did when he was a kid. This time, though, he didn't get yelled at. His fans and All-Star teammates cheered him on.

In the first round of the playoffs, the Chicago Bulls swept the Heat. It was the first time a defending NBA champion was swept in the first round of the playoffs in fifty years.

The 2007–2008 season was even worse for Shaquille. At thirty-six, Shaq was now one of the oldest players in the league. His body was beat up. He continued to battle injuries and averaged a career low 14.2 points per game. Soon Shaquille was traded to the Phoenix Suns. He was moving back West, but it wouldn't be for long.

CHAPTER 12
Moving On with No Regrets

After Shaquille left Miami, he played single seasons for the Phoenix Suns, the Cleveland Cavaliers, and the Boston Celtics from 2008 to 2011. However, he had so many injuries, he only played fifty-three games in Cleveland alongside LeBron James and thirty-seven games with the

Shaquille playing with LeBron James
on the Cleveland Cavaliers, 2010

Celtics. All those years of getting fouled and hit had taken its toll. Shaquille was now thirty-nine years old. It was time for him to hang up his giant sneakers. He retired on June 2, 2011, after nineteen seasons in the league. During his entire career, he had been named an All-Star fifteen times.

"We did it. Nineteen years, baby," Shaquille said in a video message to his fans. "I want to thank you very much, that's why I'm telling you first, I'm about to retire. Love you, talk to you soon."

Shaquille didn't fade into the background, though. That just wasn't him. Instead, he joined the show *Inside the NBA* on the cable-TV station

TNT. He talks about the current league and its players—many times in a funny way. He also does voice-overs for cartoon characters, including Smooth Smurf in the movie *Smurfs 2* and a LEGO version of himself in *The LEGO Movie*.

Shaq also became a giant in the business world. He is seen and heard everywhere—on television, the radio, and the internet—endorsing products, including Oreos, Krispy Kreme doughnuts, auto insurance, credit cards, home security devices, and Icy Hot, a pain reliever. Icy Hot is especially

perfect for Shaquille, who had his share of pain and injuries during his career. Shaq believes in telling the truth, so he won't promote a product unless he likes it or uses it himself. "If I'm gonna sell it to the people," Shaq says, "I have to be honest with the people."

Shaquille also continues to follow his mom and stepdad's advice. He went back to school again to earn a doctorate in education from Barry University in Miami Shores, Florida. Shaq also earned another nickname with his degree—Doctor O'Neal.

Just like his parents taught him, Shaquille continues to help other people. He serves Thanksgiving meals to homeless people every year. And he continues to dress up as Shaq-a-Claus every Christmas and give toys to poor children. After a mother of one of Shaquille's fans confronted him about the high cost of NBA players' sneakers, Shaq realized that average families might not be able to afford athletic sneakers that sell for hundreds of dollars.

He decided to start his own affordable sneaker line. He insists the shoes look and feel just as good as the more expensive ones. He has sold over 150 million pairs.

Shaquille was inducted into the Naismith Memorial Basketball Hall of Fame on September 9, 2016. His children, his mom, and countless other family members were all at the ceremony. Sadly, his stepfather, Philip, had died in 2013. Although he and Shaunie were divorced by then, she was there to support him, too. While accepting the honor with a speech, Shaquille said, "When a father is quizzing his son on the great big players of the game . . . Hopefully Shaquille O'Neal's name will be in the answer."

Today, four of Shaq's children have followed in his footsteps. Son Shareef and daughter Amirah both play basketball for their father's former college, Louisiana State University. His other son, Shaqir, joined the basketball team at Texas Southern University in the fall of 2021. His youngest daughter, Me'arah, is a star on her high school team in California.

Shareef O'Neal (number 32) playing for Louisiana State University

Naismith Memorial Basketball Hall of Fame

The Basketball Hall of Fame is located in Springfield, Massachusetts. It inducted its first members in 1959, and the current building opened

in 1968. The hall is named for James Naismith, a Canadian American athlete and educator who created the game of basketball in Springfield in 1891. The Hall inducts new members every year. As of fall 2021, 401 members have been inducted.

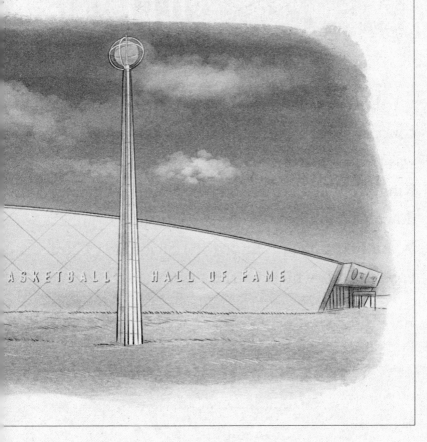

Although Shaq's own days on the basketball court are behind him, he is busier than ever. He was part owner of the NBA team the Sacramento Kings from 2013 to 2021, and currently owns a sit-down restaurant in Los Angeles called Shaquille's.

In 2019, Shaq founded the Shaquille O'Neal Foundation, which partners with the Boys and

THE SHAQUILLE O'NEAL FOUNDATION
ALL RISE

Girls Clubs of America to help underserved youth. They have donated $10 million in supplies to schools across the country and committed $10 million in grants to Black-owned businesses.

In April 2020, Shaquille starred in his own reality television show called *Shaq Life*.

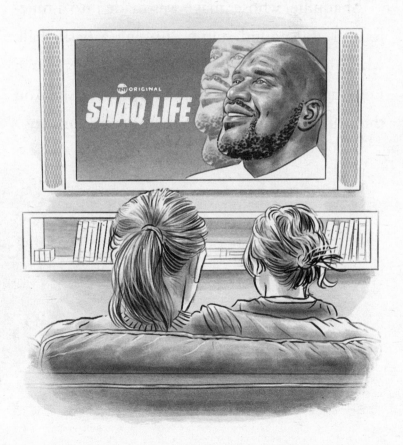

In his autobiography, *Shaq Uncut*, Shaq said people often ask him how he wants to be remembered. He always responds: "I was generous, I was dominant, I was unique. That would work." When asked by a reporter what his biggest regret was, Shaq answered, "Nothing."

Shaquille, whose image was made into a nine-foot, 1,200-pound statue dunking a basketball, which hangs outside of the Staples Center arena in Los Angeles, is celebrated not just for his skills on the court but for his larger-than-life personality.

Timeline of Shaquille O'Neal's Life

1972 — Shaquille Rashaun O'Neal is born on March 6 in Newark, New Jersey

1984 — Moves with his family to Wiesbaden, Germany

1989 — Leads Robert G. Cole High School to their first Texas state championship title

— Begins to play college basketball at Louisiana State University

1992 — Chosen by the Orlando Magic as the number one pick in the NBA Draft

1993 — Named the NBA Rookie of the Year

1996 — Joins the Los Angeles Lakers

2000 — Wins his first NBA title with the Lakers and also wins the NBA Finals MVP Award

— Graduates from Louisiana State University

2004 — Is traded to the Miami Heat

2006 — Wins an NBA title with the Miami Heat

2011 — Retires from the NBA after nineteen seasons in the league

2016 — Is inducted into the NBA Hall of Fame

2017 — Receives a bronze statue outside the Staples Center in Los Angeles, California

2019 — Founds the Shaquille O'Neal Foundation

2020 — *Shaq Life* reality television show debuts in April on TNT

Timeline of the World

1972 — United States swimmer Mark Spitz wins seven gold medals at the Summer Olympics

1975 — Tennis player Arthur Ashe becomes first Black man to win Wimbledon

1977 — *Star Wars* movie released

1985 — Wreck of the ship RMS *Titanic* found

1995 — Million Man March to promote African American unity is held in Washington, DC

1997 — First Harry Potter book is released in the United Kingdom

2001 — The biggest terrorist attack in US history takes place

2005 — Hurricane Katrina floods the city of New Orleans, Louisiana

2009 — Barack Obama is sworn in as president of the United States

2012 — The first licenses for cars without drivers are granted in the state of Nevada to Google

2020 — Kobe Bryant dies in a helicopter crash on January 26

— The NBA suspends its season starting March 12 because of the worldwide coronavirus pandemic

Bibliography

*Books for young readers

*Bernstein, Ross. *Shaquille O'Neal*. Revised Edition. Minneapolis: Lerner, 2009.

*Cox, Ted. *Shaquille O'Neal: Shaq Attack*. Chicago: Children's Press, 1993.

O'Neal, Lucille, with Allison Samuels. *Walk Like You Have Somewhere to Go: My Journey from Mental Welfare to Mental Health*. Nashville, Tennessee: Thomas Nelson, 2010.

O'Neal, Shaquille. *Shaq Talks Back*. New York: St. Martin's Press, 2001.

O'Neal, Shaquille, with Jack McCallum. *Shaq Attaq! My Rookie Year*. New York: Hyperion, 1993.

O'Neal, Shaquille, with Jackie MacMullan. *Shaq Uncut: My Story*. New York: Grand Central Publishing, 2011.

Websites

Boys & Girls Clubs of America: www.bgca.org

The Naismith Memorial Basketball Hall of Fame: www.hoophall.com

The Shaquille O'Neal Foundation: www.shaqfoundation.org